# Prepping for Disaster

## *Learn How to Survive Through the Worst Disasters*

## By Bill Shepherd

© 2015

**Are You Prepared? For almost anything?**

You know you need to be prepared. But maybe you don't know where to start? Maybe you consider yourself an expert prepper already. Maybe you're just a beginner. No matter how long you've been prepping, we all make mistakes. It's natural. It's human. But there are ways you can learn from others and avoid the same mistakes that we all make.

With this book, you'll learn how to be prepared for almost any event and how to survive for as long as you need to!

If you are interested in learning how to protect your family from any and all of the inevitable disasters that could potentially happen, this book is your first step to learning how to prepare for any emergency situation.

Don't wait - Get started today!

# Introduction

We've all seen in on the news, from all over the world. An earthquake. A hurricane. An overthrow of the government. Armed citizens in the streets. Looting. Rioting. The list of bad things that can happen on any given day is almost endless. So what can you do?

Millions of Americans are now looking to prepare themselves for what the world has to throw at them. As crazy as it sounds, this isn't such a bad idea because, in today's world, you can never truly know what is waiting around the next corner.

It may be a scary thought for some but the world is a scary place and while most of us will remain relatively safe, many will not. Unfortunately there are disasters and they come with their own hidden dangers. However, being prepared for those dangers could potentially be the difference between living and dying.

Maybe you've already started prepping. Maybe you know you *need* to start, but you don't know *where* to start. If so, then this book is exactly what you need to begin your prepping journey and be truly ready to face anything that comes your way. Prepping doesn't have to mean living in an underground bunker full of bottled water, canned foods, and every weapon you can get your hands on. Prepping comes in all shapes and sizes and can be tailored for what you and your family really need. Prepping means different things to different people, and that's exactly the way you should approach it.

You may believe you're prepared for anything but are you *really* prepared? Let's get started.

## Chapter One: Why Do You Need To Prepare For Emergencies And Natural Disasters?

Natural disasters and global emergencies aren't as rare as we think. Each year, there are thousands of disasters across the world and while most remain fairly minor, they still can be very deadly. Every disaster has its own pitfalls and those affected find themselves unprepared for the events. We see it on the news most nights, but we always think it couldn't happen to us. This is where we are wrong, and this is where prepping begins.

A weather storm may be predicted but you can't truly know the devastation it will cause; it's the same with a terror attack. An attack might be deadly but you can't predict or know how it will impact on your life or safety. Unfortunately, no one can predict what will happen even with the fancy security systems and weather forecast stations. Mother Nature is too unpredictable and, sometimes, everything comes down to human error. It might seem hopeless if you stop thinking there. But there *are* things you can do, steps you can take, to greatly increase your security and make sure that you and your family survive and thrive, no matter the situation.

In the end, being prepared for any eventuality allows you and those around you to take real steps to survive any horrors that might come your way as best as you possibly can.

**Is Prepping Really Necessary?**

This is a question that a lot of people ask, and a lot of preppers find themselves having to answer. Prepping is something very few people understand simply because they think it's a morbid or unnatural thought however, that is far from the truth. Preparing for disasters or government breakdown can be one of the smartest moves anyone can make today, simply because you're preparing for the worst.

This isn't about you *looking* for something awful to happen but rather, it's about preparing yourself and your family for anything, should a terrible tragedy occur. Disasters come in many forms, from tornadoes to terrorism and they occur at the least likely of times. Your home might appear safe but once disaster strikes, will it remain a safe haven?

No one wants to believe that anything bad will ever happen to them and their loved ones. Especially not when there is so much security out there. But, in a blink of an eye, the best security defenses can be torn down and left exposed. Thousands, if not millions, of people all around the world are not prepared for even the most minor of disasters, never mind the major ones. Sometimes, the minor disasters can cause the most problems and yet, most believe they're safe, when in reality, they are exposed to the worst elements possible.

Being unprepared is almost like ringing the dinner bell in a shark-feeding pen; you wouldn't want to be there when they come to feed. Being unprepared is simply asking for trouble. Prepping for disaster can appear to be an unnecessary and unhealthy obsession but no matter who you are or where you live, you must be fully prepared for any disaster that hits.

**What Would Your First Thoughts Be When Tragedy Hits?**
Take a moment to think about what your first thoughts or actions would be if and when a terrible disaster struck. Would you try to shore up the defenses in your home if you saw a local flood warning on TV or would you be scrambling for supplies and fighting through the crowds at the supermarket for the last bag of chips and bottled water? Would you leave your home when a terrorist attack happened in the State or would you seek shelter when a hurricane was heading your way?

The very first actions you take in a matter of seconds could determine your fate. No one thinks one hundred percent clearly at first when they hear about a minor flood or terror attack but being prepared allows you to get the shock out the way and get down to action. You will have things rehearsed and, though you will still be surprised or in shock, you will quickly revert to what you know, what you have trained for, and what you have taught yourself.

Your first instincts always will center on protecting the people and things that matter to you the most. However, sometimes, the warnings come too late and all you have is a few moments to decide your next move. When you're unprepared, you tend to make all of the wrong decisions because you spend most of the time packing up unnecessary belongings or calling around searching for help when you should just get out.

It is these simple precious seconds that could change the course of your life.

Everyone needs to be prepared so that if there is ever a time when they must survive without electricity or having drinking water, they know how to carry on and survive. Being prepared isn't something so-called crazy 'end-of-the-world' preachers are doing; everyday 9-5 people work to prepare fall-out shelters and are even ready to leave their home in a minute's notice.

Yes, it's very scary to think the worst can happen but the way you react will change everything and if you're unprepared, it's a nightmare.

**Relying On Government Assistance Might Not Be a Possibility**
Government responses during emergencies can be phenomenally good, but, as we saw with Hurricane Katrina, it comes much too late in some instances. This isn't designed to scare you because while the government has an excellent response time, it doesn't guarantee you food shelter or safety. Simply put: you can't rely on the government to take care of you in a disaster situation.

Major disasters cause a great deal of problems for the government, both on a local level and on a federal level. Roads can become inaccessible and resources might be very tight. The unfortunate truth is that while the government pulls out every stop possible to help those affected by whatever tragedy strikes, there can be time delays and lack of communication, resulting in problems for us average citizens.

Any rescue worker will understand how difficult it is to reach everyone in danger and you must understand that too, because you cannot solely rely on the government to help you. They may be able to provide additional shelter for you as well as food and water but when will that be? It could be days or possibly even weeks before you receive help and that could be too late. Do you really want to leave your survival in the hands of someone else?

The fault doesn't lie with the government or with the local police, fire and ambulance service; it's just an unfortunate trap that accompanies tragedy. You have to remember, thousands may be waiting for help but there may not be enough resources for everyone. This is why you *must* be prepared to take care of yourself and your loved ones. If you don't, who will?

However, crisis' can bring out the best in people too because those able can lend a hand to help dig out people buried in rubble and race to people struggling to stay afloat in flooded waters. Food parcels can be organized and local shelters are set up; and while this is a wonderful show of strength and community, they don't always arrive quickly.

Every situation is different, whether you're left facing a bush-fire in the Californian desert or a tornado whisking its way to Detroit. However, most think they should just prepare for natural disasters or terrorism and nothing else. But, clearly, this isn't the case, because rioting, civil violence and even simple power cuts can cause major incidents too. You have to be as prepared for civil violence as prepared for a terrorist attack or a natural disaster, because they can all be just as deadly and as frightening.

Getting support, food and shelter to every person affected can be a challenge, especially in remote areas. Sometimes, the minor incidents don't get contributions from the State as bigger incidents do. Governments can help but they aren't always able to and that is one of the biggest reasons why you must think about ways to help protect yourself and those around you.

## Chapter Two: The Essentials to Prepare For a Natural Disaster and Stay Safe

Natural disasters are as unpleasant as they are unpredictable. Sometimes, what looks like an average storm suddenly turns into a wild and deadly disaster and it's these events you have to be prepared for. Will you know what to do when Mother Nature strikes? Of course you will, because you're a prepper! And if you're prepared, you'll be far ahead of the 95% of the population who will have no idea what to do.

### Finding Shelter and Water Supplies

The body is a complicated thing because while it can go potentially weeks without food, it simply must have water to survive. You may be able to go a day or two without water but then, slowly and surely, the body starts to feel the impact. Dehydration begins to kick in and then the full force of water starvation is felt. Dehydration poses a significant risk to life and when you drink dirty water, it can cause severe health problems too. So how to prepare?

During natural disasters, it's especially difficult to find a supply of safe drinking water. However, you can avoid the struggle for water by stocking up your home. You can easily buy three or four gallons of bottled water from a local store and keep it safely in a storage cupboard until it's needed.

If you live in an area which floods annually, then it's especially a good idea to have your own supply of drinking water. It will come in quite handy, should the local supply be cut off or be unsafe to consume.

However, for shelter, you need to choose a suitable location to stay during the crisis. Ideally you want to remain indoors and your home is the best bet. Sometimes, it won't be safe to stay in if there is severe flooding or hurricanes approaching. For minor disasters such as power cuts and light hail storms, the home is probably the safest option possible.

If you choose the home as your shelter you need to inspect the property and see what shape it's in. There may be a few upgrades needed to help keep the home safe during violence storms and if that is the case, don't be afraid to spend the money to protect the home. Hopefully you'll never need shelter but if you do, then the home is there and ready.

However, if the home isn't a safe option or you wish to have a secondary shelter in place, you could choose a local community center, a friend's home, a family member residence or even a bunker. There are lots of good options open to you so don't be afraid to explore all possibilities and find the safest shelter available to you.

**Setting up a P.O.A**

A P.O.A. or plan of action has become one of the best if not, basic survival tools to have to survive a natural disaster. These plans are great because you cover escape routes, shelters and the steps you'd take to protect yourself when a storm is brewing. However, this can be used for any disaster and creating a plan can be very easy to do.

The first step to prepare your Plan of Action would be to assess your home. There could potentially be several high-risk factors lurking around your home and these factors need to be addressed and dealt with quickly. So, let's say you lived in an area where bush-fires broke out occasionally; you would want to assess your property and the surrounding area.

Do you have any overgrown shrubbery or trees that might catch fire? Is there excessive rubbish on the property that could cause a fire to spread? It's these types of things that need to be assessed and addressed quickly when it comes to preparing and possibly even avoiding disaster.

**Protecting Property**

As much as you want to protect the items inside your home, you also need to think about outside. If there is any garden furniture outside, you have to either bring it in or secure it down so that it cannot cause any damage. Garbage cans and heavy potted plants may need to be placed indoors to prevent them from flying into cars and properties. Anything outside that isn't nailed down should be brought inside and secured in a room; of course, some items aren't suitable for indoors but those items would need to be secured as best as you possibly can outdoors.

For vehicles and automobiles, it would be much wiser to lock them up safely in the garage to keep any damage to a minimal. If you do not have a garage, you need to find a safe location for the vehicle so that it doesn't get damaged; you could always park the car in an elevated spot if flooding is predicted.

Windows and doors also need to stay locked and bolted. All shutters need to be closed and the blinds and drapes must be closed too. For heavy winds or storms, you could even look to boarding the windows and doors up with heavy wooden boards to help prevent them from breaking and shattering. Doors can be braced up with heavier objects during heavy storms; however, you could look at impact resistant window glass. Impact resistant windows are a lot more expensive but they can be quite effective at the same time.

If there is flooding expected, it would be much better to start moving items from the lower floors of the home into the second floor. Valuables can be stored in rooms higher up and expensive furniture can be moved upstairs or somewhere the water cannot get to it. This should also include your insurance documents – these should be stored in a water and fireproof locked box in a dry location.

**Create Your Emergency Kit**

You cannot prepare for a disaster without creating an emergency kit. This is an essential part of surviving because should you ever have to leave your home, you have the emergency kit all ready and waiting. There are companies who pre-make emergency kits but it's much better to build one yourself.

This isn't stocking up a huge pile of food or water but rather the necessary items you'll need during an emergency. When preparing your kit, have a three-day supply of fresh and preferably warm clothing as well as several maps of the local area. There should also be a flashlight with extra batteries, a battery-powered radio, a first aid kit, blankets, sanitation items; and there should be food and water rations for at least three days. A whistle can also be useful to attract help.

To be honest, an emergency kit can grow and grow but you should just have the bare essentials so it can be picked up and moved quickly. You might need to go on the move and you can't have an emergency kit that weighs hundreds of pounds otherwise, you won't get far.

It can also be a good idea to have an emergency kit stored in your car just in case a disaster strikes when you're out of the home. The car kit can basically hold the same items with the exception of maybe spare cash to help find a safe way home.

## Have a First Aid Kit for Injuries

A first aid kit can be so useful to have at hand when someone is hurt and help can't get through. Of course, a first aid kit isn't going to offer the same type of equipment a doctor has but it will offer some of the essential items. You can have a good stock of medical bandages, sterile dressings, antibiotic hand wash, a thermometer, simple aspirin and pain relief medicines and scissors medical tape.

All of these items can be very important to have during a natural disaster for minor cuts and injuries. The kit might just allow you to help someone until medical help is able to get to you.

## Always Carry Extra Fuel for the Car

You can't predict what you'll need to do during a crisis and it might be that leaving your home is a must. However, your vehicle absolutely must be fully gassed up at all times. You can't stop off at gas stations to fill up because they will be a nightmare and it's quite possible, there will be no gas or fuel available in miles.

Instead, you can store anything up to twenty gallons for an emergency. However, the gas shouldn't be stored anywhere inside the home for safety. Keep the extra fuel in a safe location where only you know of it.

## Communication Is a Must

Most people own a cell phone today and you must have at least one fully charged up phone with you at all times no matter where you go. It might be a good idea to buy a second cheap but reliable cell phone and store it in the car or in an emergency kit should you ever need it. Also, keep a second charger in the emergency kit.

Landlines can be just as good as cell phones, if not a little more reliable however, they might not be working still which is why a cell phone is a must. However, phones aren't the only options to consider to keep in contact with the outside world you can also use computers.

**Prepare the Home**

You will need a supply of food for the upcoming days, if not weeks, which means you have to do a lot of stocking up. Now, water can be bought over time and stored until it's needed but for foods, it's a little different because some can go out-of-date quickly. So, it's best to stick with canned goods as well as simple everyday foods such as crackers and cereals and even chocolate bars.

Should the power go out and you're stuck in home, you have a few options for food. For the refrigerator items, you can eat them first as long as you eat them within the first few hours of the power going off. For any food item that looks questionable, don't eat it. After three or four hours, the food in the refrigerator might not be good enough to eat so dispose of them and move onto your canned goods and long lasting snacks.

Frozen foods can still be consumed but it's not always advisable. If you plan to eat meat that's thawing from the freezer, it should be cooked thoroughly and consumed immediately. However, if the power has been off for a considerable amount of time, you should not consume any foods whatsoever for safety reasons. Sometimes, it's best to stick to your food rations.

Another important factor to remember is checking on your fire blankets and extinguishers regularly. Now, these items should be stored at various points in the home and they need to be checked on ever few months. If you can, have a fire extinguisher or fire blanket on every floor in the home and possibly every room especially in high-risk areas such as the kitchen.

When the electricity goes out, you are going to have very limited options. You cannot use any electric item, which means it's difficult to get a read on the events outside because if the modem is down you can't get online. You can still use battery-powered radios, which will give you some necessary updates so remember to have your radios at the ready.

**Have Cash at the Ready**

Stashing a huge sum of cash in the home isn't always a good idea but it's a wise move to have a little cash ready. Emergencies can often lead to a rush to the local ATM machines and in a panic, banks can be closed for several reasons, which could potentially leave you with little or no cash. However, if you have a small amount of cash in your home, you have at least something to use.

**Get To Higher Ground and Stay Safe**

For areas that receive severe flooding, it would be best to look for higher ground. If you are staying within your home, you should retreat to the upper floors. It might not be wise to head into the attic unless you feel totally safe about that area of the home. However, if you aren't staying within the home due to rising floodwaters, you need to find safety with higher ground. You can head to local shelters or areas which are safe from flood waters but remember to stay safe when evacuating your home.

When the storm hits outside, you should find the safest room within your shelter. Ideally, the room would have little or no windows and it would have enough space to hold the family comfortably until the crisis is over. There should be at least one room in the home or shelter that is suitable to ride the storm out.

Do not use any form of electricity when it comes to a natural disaster. If there is flooding, no matter how minor it could cause serious injury to you and may lead to fire. Also, if you're leaving the home, follow all safety instructions and find the safest and quickest route out.

## Get Insurance

Everyone has their own thoughts about insurance and while most will have some sort of insurance on the property or valuables, you might not. It's really your choice whether or not you want to insure your property; it could be a good idea but it's down to you. If your home is regularly flooded then insurance prices might be higher but you'll have to do some checking.

# Chapter Three: How to Survive Civil Violence and Power Outages

Pandemonium can break out at the least expected of times and while your hometown might appear safe, the situation can change quickly. Civil unrest and violence occurs more than you think and it can have huge repercussions for all involved even if you aren't directly involved with any violence. A simple power shortage might even cause civil unrest to break out and you must know how to survive.

## Stock Up On Supplies When You Hear Of Problems

If you have an emergency kit already stored in your home, that can be very useful but civil unrest and violence can carry on for weeks at a time. You will need more supplies so, whenever you hear of unrest at the next town over, it's time to get stocked up. It's the same if you hear about upcoming marches or protests in your local area; your first port of call should be to the local grocery store and then the hardware store.

It doesn't hurt to spend a little extra cash on supplies such as canned goods, energy bars, protein bars, crackers, jams, jellies, canned fruits and simple snacks that are long lasting. There are plenty of good foods out there that last a considerable time so look for things you and your family will eat – and don't forget extra bottled water!

However, don't make it obvious you're stocking up on supplies because word will get out and there'll be a panic. Instead, casually shop and if that means going to a few stores, so be it; just make sure you have enough food and water supplies to last for the upcoming days. Remember, civil violence and even a power cut can last week's so be prepared for longer problems.

**Plan Your Home Route**

When a power shortage strikes or violence breaks out, it would be much easier to lock the doors and stay inside until the chaos passes but what happens if you or your family are out? Well, it can be a very frightening time but if you ever find yourself away from the home during civil violence, you have to plan your next move.

Ideally you want to get back home to where it's safe or to where your family is, so you want to set out your plan to get home. You know the local area and you probably already know what routes you'll take when you're at work or the shops but the direct routes mightn't be possible to take. You will need to have several back-up routes home so that when disaster strikes, you can safely find your way home.

Everyone in your family should have their own routes devised so that they are able to make their way home safely and without being caught up in the violence. Of course, you would prefer to be locked safely indoors when a power cut happens or when civil unrest breaks-out but it isn't always going to be that way. However, when you devise your safety routes home, you will hopefully avoid danger as best as you can.

Don't be afraid to learn the home routes by heart and if you have to, go on dry runs so you can get the routes planted in your mind for whenever you need them. Every member of your family should do this and don't forget to add a route to school to pick up the children. Younger children shouldn't be heading out alone during civil unrest and even some older children shouldn't be venturing out alone either.

## Ditch the Car When You're Faced with Roaming Dangers and Blocked Roads

Experts say it's best to stay where you are during civil unrest because it's too dangerous to go outdoors. However, it isn't a wise idea to sit in your car in the middle of civil unrest either, especially when there are mobs romancing the streets. Mobs can be very dangerous and while they aren't there to intentionally cause you harm, you might inadvertently get in the way.

Things can spiral out of control very quickly and you don't want to be there when a mob turns on you or your vehicle. You don't want to leave your car behind but if the road becomes blocked, congested or impassible, then it's time to ditch the car and head on home on foot.

If you can, store a backpack with an emergency cell phone, some cash, water and a map of the local area. They will help get your home and remember to lock up the car; it might not do a great deal to protect it but if you can, park it in a safe area if possible.

**Seek Shelter from Safety**

Power cuts and civil unrest can be very much the same – looters come out to play as well as a lot of unsavory characters – and being caught amongst them can be scary. If you find yourself away from the safety of your home, you need to try and find shelter; somewhere that is safe and secure from trouble brewing outside.

You could seek shelter at a family or colleague's home or even at a local community center; police stations might be a bit chaotic but most police officers are willing to help innocent people trying to seek shelter from the violence outside. Even in a power cut, police officers would be willing to offer a helping hand to those stuck with no means of getting home.

If you find yourself far away from the home and no other shelters are available, you still need to keep a low profile. Try to stay away from crowded areas and take a safe route home; if you are really stuck in the middle of nowhere, seek shelter where you can, even if that means ducking in and out of alleyways and abandoned buildings. Ideally you'd have a shelter in place but if not, don't panic and seek shelter where you can.

## Stay Indoors At All Costs

Going outside when there is a riot or power cut outside can be very, very dangerous for you. You could put yourself in harm's way by getting caught up in rioting, violence and even looting; you certainly do not want to be there when that happens. It's best for you and your family's safety to stay inside.

The best move for you is to hunker down in your shelter. You should lock and secure all doors and windows and board up any potential entry also. For those living in a condo or an apartment should maybe consider adding double locks to the doors and windows and even maybe blocking the entry points with heavy objects so that should someone try to gain entry, they won't be able to. Barricading yourself in might be extreme but if things get out of control, it's a possibility – just remember to remain indoors at all times.

## Stock Up On Medicines and Medical Supplies

You don't know how long you're going to be stuck indoors when civil violence breaks-out and you have to be prepared for every possible problem. It would be a good idea to have all of the family's prescriptions filled and up-to-date and stored so that you don't run out of much needed and potentially life-saving medication or medicines.

Also, you have to think about having an extra supply of medical bandages, disposable gloves, hand gels, plasters and all other necessary medical supplies. Your emergency kit should have your first aid kits but if you choose not to opt for the emergency kit, try to set up your own home first aid kit to deal with injuries. The most important point to remember is stocking up on prescriptions such as allergy medicines, diabetes medication and other life-threatening medications.

**Avoid Crowded Areas and the Hot Zone**
The number one rule to deal with civil violence is to avoid overly crowded areas! The hot zone is going to be at the epicenter of the chaos and you do not want to find yourself in these areas whatsoever. The hot zone presents the worst of the worst trouble and being caught here can be very dangerous for you to deal with.

Instead, do your best to avoid the hot zone and crowded areas as much as possible. However, if you do find yourself in crowded areas that are full of trouble, you need to keep a level head. Don't get caught up in the chaos; try to slip away from these areas and get indoors and stay there until the trouble is over.

**Don't Resist Arrest if you're caught Up With Protesters**
Hopefully you'll be indoors but if you somehow manage to find yourself outside and in the middle of a riot, you have to be smart. Police are going to be swarming everywhere and if you find yourself

being taken into custody, don't struggle and don't resist! The charges might just be breach of the peace but if you struggle or try to resist you might get additional charges that are much worse.

As said, you really should be indoors but if you get caught up while on the way home, follow the officers instructions at all times. The best advice for being outdoors – don't be there!

**Be Wary Of Roadblocks**

When there is severe civil violence outside, there can be checkpoints and roadblocks set up along the major highways and roads to help stamp out looters and protesters. However, some checkpoints might not have been set up by police, but rather, by those looking for trouble. If you can, avoid the roadblocks as much as possible.

**Have a Back-Up Plan in Place**

If your home is a no-go area or right in the epicenter, you might be best to seek alternative shelter. It might simply not be safe to head back home for the foreseeable future and if that's the case, you have to find another shelter, which is safe for you to remain in which the disruptions outside continue.

It might be possible to seek shelter with a neighbor, a family member or even a friend. There should always be a back-up plan in place when you need shelter and even if it's taking cover at the local library, so be it, as long as it's safe.

**Avoid Everyone and Trust Your Instincts**

During unrest there can be a lot of mobs, gangs and groups around looking to cause trouble and you want to avoid them all. In fact, during crisis times, you really want to avoid as much people as possible, if not them all because any one person can be dangerous. It's crazy to say but a person can react completely different during a riot than what they would during a normal day and its best to avoid everyone.

Also, your instincts might tell you to do one thing and you should follow those instincts because they might just help to keep you safe. If your instincts are telling you to remain indoors, do it; or if they're telling you to avoid making a lot of noise, don't make any noise!

**Putting Up Defenses for Your Home As Long As You Can**

How you choose to defend your home depends entirely on your thoughts and feelings. While you might have a right to bear arms and protect your family, it's your choice whether that is right for you. To be honest, some people will say they don't want firearms in their home and that is up to them and their right; and vice versa for those who want to carry arms. However, if you should choose to defend your home using a weapon, please be very careful with it and most importantly understand how to use it.

If you choose not to carry a weapon, you can still defend the home. For a start, you should secure every possible entry point from the garage door to the basement window. There are dozens of potential entry points and you must secure them all; it might sound a little stupid but your doggy doors needs to be fairly secured as well. You can easily board up the windows from the outside as well as on the inside too, close the shutters on the outside and barricade the doors.

However, if you are not able to defend the home for whatever reason, have your escape route planned. Don't put yourself in harm's way to save your home because it could cost you your life so use the best judgment and if you feel it's time to leave, find a safe exit and head towards another shelter if you can.

**Staying Safe Inside during a Power Cut or Riot**

It's very easy to say that since you live in a remote area, its unlikely major rioting will flare up and while that is possible, it's not a guarantee. What is more, even if there isn't violence where you reside that doesn't mean the impact from the rioting in major cities won't eventually cause disruption for you. Remote areas can at times be hit hard even when it isn't affected directly by violence; you cannot be complacent into believing there won't be any disruption to food or water supplies.

Also, if you plan to travel anywhere in the local or wider communities, you need to research how safe the areas are. Keep a close eye on proceedings locally and on a broad aspect too so that you can be totally sure how safe the towns and cities are. It would help to keep an eye over weather conditions too.

Whether you plan to travel or just want to prepare for impending disaster, it's important to keep an eye out for signs. Now, some signs might be very obvious and on television there are threats of violence made and if you spot trouble brewing, get your supplies at the ready.

# Chapter Four: Creating the Perfect Bug-Out Bag

Leaving your home in a second's notice can be very tense. However, a bug-out bag can become the number one tool to rely on during a disaster. Though, hundreds of people aren't really sure what they need to equip with their bug-out bag. So, what should you kit your bug-out bag with?

## How to Create Your Bug-Out Bag

Ideally your bug-out bag should contain enough supplies and materials to last you for the upcoming days. You might need to leave the home for days at a time and it needs to be well stocked and prepared for any occasion.

The bug-out bag may be a little heavier than an emergency kit but you are using more than just the basic supplies. The bag should have enough items for surviving between eight and ten days outside the home. Now, you can go all out and get very serious here and stock up with tons and tons of emergency supplies but, let's face it, it's difficult to take it all with you anywhere. The bug-out bag is designed to be easy to carry but effectively kitted out so don't go crazy and overstuff the bag with unnecessary items.

The best place to start your bug-out bag is with the food and water supply. You need at least one liter of water each day, so you should have four or five liters of bottled water in your bag. If you plan to get water from other sources outside the home, you'll need to use a water filter system to help make it safe to drink. Now, you could choose the old-fashioned means of boiling the water with iodine tablets which would sanitize the water and make it suitable to consume. For this method, you'll need to have a pack of iodine tablets and a small saucepan – and don't forget the safety matches!

For foods, canned goods such as canned meat, tuna, canned fruits and peanut butter make great items to opt for. However, you can also choose quinoa, barley, kidney beans, lentils, pasta and cornmeal too; and powdered milk and candy can also be suitable options. Of course, canned goods can be heavy so you might want to look at packet foods and only pack three or four canned items. You can add more if you are able to carry more but don't overload the bag with canned foods; and remember to take along light cooking equipment such as a skillet or saucepan.

The bag must also be equipped with a tent or warm blankets; and you should also have a thick tarp to shield you from rain, sleet and snow. There may come a time when you have to sleep outdoors or spend a period outside and you must have some form of shelter to help protect you from the elements. Even if you have a tent, you can still take a tarp with you and prop it up and it can act as a shelter.

Next, you must have two or three changes of suitable, warm clothing with you. Ideally you would have two or three warm jumpers, a few pairs of thick or durable pants and a few pairs of t-shirts or undershirts and clean underwear. However, you cannot forget about suitable footwear. You should have thick, heavy boots suitable for any and all road conditions. Men and women can both use walking boots and remember to ditch less durable footwear like sneakers and high heels.

All bug-out bags need to have some sort of first aid kits. Now, you can easily pick up a kit from a local pharmacy or make one from scratch. If you don't want to spend the time putting together your own first aid kit then buy a basic kit and add it into your bag.

Don't forget to pack additional maps of the local area!

**Prepare and Keep Your Bag Close**

Now you know how to prepare your bug-out bag, it's time to let you in on a few secrets. One of the biggest errors most people make is to know how to prepare their bags but don't get around assembling it. Now, while you might think you'll have time to sort everything out later on, you might find that's a terrible idea. You can't know what is coming around the corner and it might be that you don't have three minutes so your bag must be ready and all prepared.

You can't be rushing around throwing your bug-out bag together; it should be packed and stored safely, somewhere you can easily get to it. If you can, create a second bug-out bag and store it in the car of the office should you be unable to get home for it. Occasionally update the bag to check on the food and throw in new clothes if you outgrow your clothes.

Remember, the whole point of the bug-out bag is to leave with it in seconds so don't go putting it somewhere you can't get to it.

**Create A Meeting Place during an Emergency**

Bugging out in a matter of seconds can be made a lot simpler once you have a plan of escape set up. Now, you probably know all the escape routes in your home but what about after you leave, where will you go? Well, this is something you have to prepare for because if you have no central meeting point then you'll be going around in circles.

Remember, internet and phone lines may be down and if you're separated from your family members, then at least you all know where your meeting place is. Your location can be something as simple as your front lawn or even a town hall; but no matter where your meeting point is, ensure everyone knows how to get to it. There is no point in creating an escape plan without having a meeting place in mind.

Minor emergencies need escape plans and a safe meeting location just as the major emergencies. However, when you're creating your escape plan and meeting place, try to ensure it's going to be safe for everyone to get to. It might be a good idea to have a central meeting point where every family member knows about as well as a second meeting place that can be used as a fallback position.

**Don't Delay In Leaving**

Your bugging out for a reason – it's dangerous to stay where you are – so don't delay in moving out. Yes, it's hard to leave everything you own behind but for safety, you have to. You never know, when you return, the home might still be in the same position as you left it but you can't delay leaving when there is a major disaster.

If you hear the three-minute warning or if a hurricane is heading your way, get out! Take your bug-out bag, get into your car and leave as fast as you can.

**Set Up Several Evacuation Routes for Leaving Your Home**

There are usually a few major roads leading in and out of a town and while your first thought is to take these routes – think again. When a major incident occurs and everyone is heading out of town, all of the major routes out will be backlogged and chock full of vehicles and people looking to escape the disaster. These routes aren't going to be accessible at the best of times and you need to search for alternative routes.

It's vital to have several escape routes planned and set out. You could look at the minor or smaller routes to take you out of the city, which might take you a little longer to leave, but they could be worth their weight in gold. You should have one alternative route set out and if that one fails to work out, have another and another. Ideally, you should have several evacuation routes set up so that if one or two fails, there is always another back-up road out.

Of course, if you know your way around the local area then you probably already know what routes to take. If you don't know the local area, its best to keep a map with you at all times and consult it should an emergency arise when you're out and about or travelling to an unknown area.

## Chapter Five: Surviving Any Disaster – What Steps To Take To Keep the Family Safe

Your family is the people you care about most of all. You would do anything for them and you'd ensure their safety no matter what but how would you keep them safe during a crisis? You might have a plan for the local weather but what happens when a Nation-wide disaster strikes, would you still be able to keep your family safe?

Don't panic, because there are hundreds of other families in the same boat as you and while it may be a scary task to keep your family protected, it doesn't need to be impossible. Here are some simple but effective ways to help prepare your family for the worst events imaginable and help keep them safe.

### Be Prepared For a Terror Attack

There is no simple or mathematical theory to predict an act of terrorism, unfortunately. This is one of the worst atrocities and yet, you can be prepared should it ever happen near you. It might not be easy but you can always be prepared for whatever comes your way.

If your local town, city or district suddenly finds itself the center of a terror attack, the best thing for you to do is lock your doors and stay inside. Now, if you live on the edge of town, it's unlikely you'll be affected as much as those who live in the epicenter. However, if you live a fair distance away from the attack, you should remain indoors and secure the building whether it's in the form of a chemical attack or any other attack.

For those who live within the epicenter of the attack, you have a few options; the first being evacuating the home. Now, evacuation might not be necessary unless your home is at risk from the effects of the attack or that it's simply not safe for you to remain there. If that is the case, grab your bug-out bag or emergency kit and leave and get to safety. You can take shelter at a local hospital if you require treatment or stay with a family member if you aren't hurt.

The second option for you would be to remain indoors. Now, this might be a solution if it's unsafe to leave the home. If you cannot leave then hunker down in the home and secure all doors and windows until help arrives. This might not be the best solution but if its unsafe to go outside, you must remain protected at all times.

If an attack occurs while you're out of the home or out of the city, you will need to get out of the danger zone. This can be often difficult don't try not to panic. It's easier said than done I know however, in these awful times, its best to keep your head so that you can get out of the danger zone and head to safety.

For those who plan to get out of the city or the danger zone, you have to be wary of the local area. Buildings might be unstable so, watch for falling debris and be wary of any unsavory characters. If you wish to stay and help those who have been hurt, that's great on you but you still need to remain vigilant.

## Head to Your Fall-Out Shelter after Biological or Chemical Incidents

Fall-out shelters have become such a driving force of late and more and more people are now choosing to buy one especially for their family. You could always make a little purchase of a fall-out shelter and during biological or chemical incidents, retreat to here.

It's a good place to ride out the storm and hopefully you'll remain safe there. However, if you are going to use a fall-out shelter, take some supplies for the upcoming weeks and have battery powered radios to keep up-to-date with the latest news.

### Evacuate the Town If Necessary

It isn't just necessary to evacuate when a terrorist attack strikes but also some natural disasters. For a start, violent thunderstorms and severe flooding might call for you to evacuate the local area. If this is something the government or local authority advises, do so quickly but calmly.

Follow the State's advice and don't delay in getting out. If you don't have any transport to leave, the government might be able to organize public transport and if you are considered a vulnerable person, there should be some organized help for you to evacuate.

However, if you can, band up with a neighbor or family member and pull resources together.

**Work With Vulnerable People And Give Them A Leg Up!**
There are lots of vulnerable people out there from elderly residents to handicap individuals and when there is a disaster; they may find it considerably harder to stay safe. Now, the local authorities can't help everyone however, if you see anyone in need of help or know-of someone who may need additional help, why not offer your services? There is no harm in going around to a neighbor and check on their safety and well being.

This isn't about earning brownie points or gold stars but rather ensuring the safety of others around you.

**Secure Up the Home**
Inspect the home in regular periods. Check on every inch of the home from the foundations to the roof and everything in-between. You want to ensure the home has no faults and if there is anything which might need to be repaired to help secure the home, do it.

There are plenty of ways to help secure the home too including having impact resistant glass on the windows and extra locks on the door. A dead-bolt can be good to help when there is rioting outside as well as storm storms and winds and keeping outdoor furniture indoors during storms or securing them down.

**Use Coolers to Store Foods during Blackouts**

When the power goes out, you have a few options to keep your perishable yogurts, cheeses and dairy products fresh. The best and only real option would be to use a cooler but again, these would only work for a few hours after the fridge goes out. However, if you can, eat as much food that is going to get spoiled within the first few hours so that it doesn't all go to waste.

If the power is going to be off for a while, you can start off with the fridge items and then move onto your supplies within your home. You should still have your emergency rations and preserves stored away so before you start on these, you can finish off whatever you have lying around that's still edible. However, don't eat anything from the refrigerator after three or four hours.

To help keep open packet foods fresh, store them in sealable containers.

**Filter All Drinking Water**

For water coming straight out of a sealed bottle, you shouldn't have many problems with it; however, if you choose to get drinking water from a tap, you need to take steps to make it safe. Now, you can go the older method of boiling the water before using it or you can also buy a water filtration system, which can be very useful. These systems can be a bit costly but they can be worth it if you can get your hands on one of these.

**Use Any Alternative Power Source Available**

Backup generators have to be one of the best alternative power sources to rely on. Now, if you're lucky enough to have one, use it because it might just help to get you through the upcoming days. Backup generators can be a bit costly at the best of times but during extended blackouts or power cuts, they can be so useful.

However, you can also rely on solar energy. This isn't going to be for everyone but if you already have solar energy panels in your home then it could help to power the home until normal electrical supplies are restored.

## Chapter Six: Simple Steps to Keep the Family Safe during an Earthquake

Earthquakes are one of the most frequent disasters most towns and cities face in America today and they can be just as deadly as any other disaster out there. An earthquake might appear fairly minor but you can't predict how much damage it will cause. There have been earthquakes that cause power lines to come down as well as cause holes in roads to appear – the potential damage is unknown but very deadly.

Here are a few steps to help protect your family during and after an earthquake.

### Identify Hazards within Your Home and Property

First and foremost, you have to know what the potential hazards and dangers there are. The exterior needs to be assessed; if there is garden furniture, look to see whether it's close to the property as well as whether it's likely to do damage.

Next, head into your garage and look at where your car is parked. Are there any hanging shelves in the garage that could break and cause damage to the car? Well, if there is, you need to think about securing the shelves better or move the car to an area of the garage that doesn't have any hanging objects.

For the interior of the home, you have lots of issues on hand. Now, for ornaments and little trinkets on tables, windowsills and shelves, you can't really do much with these because you can't predict an earthquake. However, you can secure moveable objects instead such as water or boil tanks, unstable shelves and bookcases. It's strange but there are several dangerous items in your home that need to be secured better should an earthquake hit.

Take a good look around the home, inside and out; and identify what hazards there are as well as the steps to take to make the home more secure. Things will get damaged and broken but they can be easily replaced; heavier items need to be secured down as best as possible.

**Decide Your Safe Areas in the Home and Have a Plan Ready**
Mostly, when an earthquake occurs, you head into the doorways to protect yourself but you should still have designated safe areas in the home. This can be a room that doesn't have items or objects hanging on the wall. However, you should also set up an emergency plan for an earthquake just in case you find yourself unable to get to a safe location.

**Place Your Rations in Convenient Spots**
You probably have all of your supplies and rations at the ready but how easy are they to get to? It's important to keep all of your rations and supplies in convenient areas where you and your family can easily get to without venturing far. Now, if you have a one-floor

home, look at placing the rations in the master bedroom so that it's the central location.

For an up and downstairs home, you might want to store them in a central area such as a cupboard in the den or front living room. However, the supplies should be accessible for all.

## Take Cover

When an earthquake hits, you must find cover. You could stay in a doorway to avoid falling objects or if you can't get to a doorway, take cover under a strong table. Don't stand underneath shelves because you could be hurt from falling objects.

## Clean Up and Record the Incident

After the earthquake has struck, you have the duty of cleaning up whatever damage has been caused. If there is considerable damage inside, clean up and if there is damage to the property, clean up the glass, board the windows and take pictures for insurance claims.

## Chapter Seven: Survivalist Tips You Can Use In Real Life Situations

Emergencies and crisis' are never pleasant but they will come at some point. Being prepared may just allow you to avoid serious injury, if not keep your family safe. However, most people don't like to think about disasters or emergencies affecting them.

That is a stupid way to think because something will come your way at least once in your lifetime, whether it's a minor flood, an extended power cut or even (hopefully never) a terror attack. If you aren't prepared for these events, it could cost you your life so being prepared; even just a little prepared could save you or your family's life. Of course, you shouldn't go around being afraid of what will happen but at the same time, you shouldn't be totally unprepared either.

You need to have a balance between being prepared and being worried because while a disaster might come around once in your life, it's still vital to prepare for it. You could end up putting your life at serious risk just because you didn't prepare for such events.

### Don't Panic, Keep a Calm Head

It's very easy for someone to sit and say when a disaster strikes, you should remain calm but going out of your mind with fear is never good idea. You must remain as calm as possible and keep a level head, if only to help get you and your family to a safe zone.

Crazy things happen and while you might be in a safe town now, that could change in a blink of an eye. If you're unprepared for any emergency or disaster then you'll end up panicking and doing all the wrong things. Instead, take a moment to take a deep breath, assess the situation and get your thinking cap on!

**Add To Your Food Rations Whenever You Can**
Your home can have a nice little food supply cupboard all ready and prepared for when things take a turn for the worst and you shouldn't be afraid to continue to add to it. Now, you might think you have enough food but you don't know how long you might need to be indoors for and it doesn't hurt to have enough.

Of course, if some foods are about to expire then use them in your daily meals and replace them. Canned goods usually last a very long time so you probably don't have to worry too much about these. However, for backpack meals and packets of foods, you might need to take a closer look at them every so often.

Though, whenever you are out at the grocery store, why not pick up an extra item or two and add that into your ration cupboard. You should do the same with water as well as batteries and medical supplies. If you continue to do this, whenever there is an emergency you have enough supplies to see you through until help arrives or until it's safe to go outdoors.

## Have a Contingency Plan

You might have your escape and evacuation plans all set out and prepared but what happens if a spanner is thrown into the works? Well, you might need to alter the plan somewhere and if you aren't prepared for this then it can go downhill fast.

Instead, you should set out several plans so that if one should fail or be unusable, there is another to work with.

## Work With Others

It doesn't matter if you're a single person or have a family unit; you still need to consider working with the people around you. Remember, there are going to be others out there who don't have anyone to rely on and have no supplies at hand and while you may not have a huge amount yourself, it can be good to help someone in need. You shouldn't give away all you've worked for but you can share and you never know you might be able to pull in precious resources you don't have.

A group unit can have a better chance of survival than one man on his own simply because there are more resources available. You should always consider working with others whom you trust and you can rely on also.

## Disasters Happens – Don't Shy Away

Let's face it, disasters will happen whether they are major or minor and help might not come. It's your chance to sit up, take charge and survive whatever is out there. This is never going to be easy and it won't be pleasant but if you shy away or rely on others to help you, you might be in for a nasty surprise.

You have to be the person who stands up and really takes the reins so that you survive and make it to safety. It's easy to let someone else handle the work but that mightn't always be an option for you. Instead of shying away, get ready, be prepared and handle whatever disaster comes your way.

## Conclusion

Thank you to all who took the time to read this book. I hope you have enjoyed reading and know a little more about prepping for disaster.

This wasn't meant to scare anyone but rather help those wants to learn more about prepping for impending disasters as well as hopefully help anyone survive should they find themselves in a dangerous situation.

Good luck, fellow preppers!

*****

If you've enjoyed this book, **please** consider leaving a review and letting others know what you thought!